DATE DUE

DUE 3'99			

DEMCO 38-296

BY CHARLES WRIGHT

POETRY
The Grave of the Right Hand
Hard Freight
Bloodlines
China Trace
The Southern Cross
Country Music: Selected Early Poems
The Other Side of the River
Zone Journals
Xionia
The World of the Ten Thousand Things: Poems 1980–1990
Chickamauga

TRANSLATIONS
The Storm and Other Things (Eugenio Montale)
Orphic Songs (Dino Campana)

NONFICTION
Halflife
Quarter Notes

BLACK ZODIAC

BLACK ZODIAC

CHARLES WRIGHT

FARRAR, STRAUS AND GIROUX

NEW YORK

Farrar, Straus and Giroux
19 Union Square West, New York 10003

PS 3573 .R52 B47 1997

Wright, Charles, 1935-

Black zodiac

-in-Publication Data

Vright.—1st ed.

I. Title.
PS3573.R52B47   1997
811'.54—dc21   96-49508

Grateful acknowledgment is made to the following publications,
in whose pages these poems first appeared: Poetry, DoubleTake,
The Paris Review, Columbia, Field, The Gettysburg Review,
The Colorado Review, The Yale Review, Ploughshares, The
Atlanta Review, Orion, The Threepenny Review, The Iowa
Review, The New Republic, The Bellingham Review, The
American Poetry Review.

FOR GAETANO PRAMPOLINI

CONTENTS

1

APOLOGIA PRO VITA SUA

I

How soon we come to road's end—
Failure, our two-dimensional side-kick, flat dream-light,
Won't jump-start or burn us in,

Dogwood insidious in its constellations of part-charred cross
    points,
Spring's via Dolorosa
                 flashed out in a dread profusion,
Nowhere to go but up, nowhere to turn, dead world-weight,

They've gone and done it again,
                     dogwood,
Spring's sap-crippled, arthritic, winter-weathered, myth limb,
Whose roots are my mother's hair.

Landscape's a lever of transcendence—
                  jack-wedge it here,
Or here, and step back,
Heave, and a light, a little light, will nimbus your going forth:

The dew bead, terminal bead, opens out
                  onto a great radiance,
Sun's square on magnolia leaf
Offers us entrance—
        who among us will step forward,

Camellia brown boutonnieres
Under his feet, plum branches under his feet, white sky, white
    noon,
Church bells like monk's mouths tonguing the hymn?

———————

Journal and landscape
—Discredited form, discredited subject matter—
I tried to resuscitate both, breath and blood,
                                    making them whole again

Through language, strict attention—
Verona mi fe', disfecemi Verona, the song goes.
I've hummed it, I've bridged the break

To no avail.
            April. The year begins beyond words,
Beyond myself and the image of myself, beyond
Moon's ice and summer's thunder. All that.

———————

The meat of the sacrament is invisible meat and a ghostly
    substance.
I'll say.
        Like any visible thing,
I'm always attracted downward, and soon to be killed and
    assimilated.

Vessel of life, it's said, vessel of life, brought to naught,
Then gathered back to what's visible.
That's it, fragrance of spring like lust in the blossom-starred orchard,

The shapeless shape of darkness starting to seep through and
    emerge,

4

The seen world starting to tilt,
Where I sit the still, unwavering point
                              under that world's waves.

———————

How like the past the clouds are,
Building and disappearing along the horizon,
Inflecting the mountains,
                    laying their shadows under our feet

For us to cross over on.
Out of their insides fire falls, ice falls,
What we remember that still remembers us, earth and air fall.

Neither, however, can resurrect or redeem us,
Moving, as both must, ever away toward opposite corners.
Neither has been where we're going,
                              bereft of an attitude.

———————

Amethyst, crystal transparency,
                         Maya and Pharaoh ring,
Malocchio, set against witchcraft,
Lightning and hailstorm, birthstone, savior from drunkenness.

Purple, color of insight, clear sight,
Color of memory—
                    violet, that's for remembering,
Star-crystals scattered across the penumbra, hard stars.

Who can distinguish darkness from the dark, light from light,
Subject matter from story line,
                         the part from the whole
When whole is part of the part and part is all of it?

5

Lonesomeness. Morandi, Cézanne, it's all about lonesomeness.
And Rothko. Especially Rothko.
Separation from what heals us
                                    beyond painting, beyond art.

Words and paint, black notes, white notes.
Music and landscape; music, landscape and sentences.
Gestures for which there is no balm, no intercession.

Two tone fields, horizon a line between abysses,
Generally white, always speechless.
Rothko could choose either one to disappear into. And did.

———————

Perch'io no spero di tornar giammai, ballatetta, in Toscana,
Not as we were the first time,
                                    not as we'll ever be again.
Such snowflakes of memory, they fall nowhere but there.

Absorbed in remembering, we cannot remember—
Exile's anthem, O stiff heart,
Thingless we came into the world and thingless we leave.

Every important act is wordless—
                                    to slip from the right way,
To fail, still accomplishes something.
Even a good thing remembered, however, is not as good as not
    remembering at all.

———————

Time is the source of all good,
                                    time the engenderer

Of entropy and decay,
Time the destroyer, our only-begetter and advocate.

For instance, my fingernail,
                              so pink, so amplified,
In the half-dark, for instance,
These force-fed dogwood blossoms, green-leafed, defused,
                              limp on their long branches.

St. Stone, say a little prayer for me,
                              grackles and jay in the black gum,
Drowse of the peony head,
Dandelion globes luminous in the last light, more work to be
    done . . .

II

Something will get you, the doctor said,

                                  don't worry about that.
Melancholia's got me,
Pains in the abdomen, pains down the left leg and crotch.

Slurry of coal dust behind the eyes,
Massive weight in the musculature, dark blood, dark blood.
I'm sick and tired of my own complaints,

This quick flick like a compass foot through the testicle,
Deep drag and hurt through the groin—
Melancholia, black dog,

                       everyone's had enough.

———————

Dew-dangled, fresh-cut lawn grass will always smell like a golf
    course
Fairway to me, Saturday morning, Chuck Ross and I
Already fudging our scores down,

                       happy as mockingbirds in deep weeds,

The South Fork of the Holston River
Slick as a nickel before its confluence behind our backs
At Rotherwood with the North Fork's distant, blurred thunder,

Our rounds in the seventies always including mulligans,
Nudged lies, "found" lost balls, some extraordinary shots

And that never-again-to-be-repeated
                    teen-age false sense of attainment.

———————

One summer, aged 16, I watched—each night, it seemed—my
        roommate,
A college guy, gather his blanket up, and flashlight,
And leave for his rendezvous with the camp cook—
                    he never came back before dawn.

Some 40 years later I saw him again for the first time
Since then, in a grocery store, in the checkout line,
A cleric from Lexington, shrunken and small. Bearded even.

And all these years I'd thought of him, if at all, as huge
And encompassing,
Not rabbit-eyed, not fumbling a half-filled brown sack,
                    dry-lipped, apologetic.

———————

In 1990 we dragged Paris
                    —back on the gut again after 25 years—
The Boulevard Montparnasse,
La Coupole, the Select, you know, the Dôme, the Closerie de Lilas,

Up and down and back and forth.
Each night a Japanese girl would take a bath at 4 a.m.
In the room above ours,
                    each night someone beat his wife

In a room above the garage outside our window.
It rained all day for ten days.
Sleeplessness, hallucination, O City of Light . . .

———————

What sane, impossible reason could Percy Heath have made up
To talk to me, drunk, white and awe-struck,
—And tone-deaf to boot—
                    that night at the Carmel Mission?

But talk he did, uncondescending, feigning interest,
As Milt Jackson walked by and John Lewis walked by,
                                Gerry Mulligan
Slouched in one corner, Paul Desmond cool in an opposite one.

October, 1958, Monterey Jazz Festival,
First advisors starting to leave the Army Language School for
      South Vietnam,
The Pacific's dark eyelid
                    beginning to stir, ready to rise and roll back . . .

———————

During World War II, we lived in Oak Ridge, Tennessee,
Badges and gates, checkpoints, government housing, government
      rules.
One house we lived in was next door to a two-star admiral.

I learned a couple of things in the three-plus years we lived in
      Oak Ridge,
One from my first (and only) paper route, the second
After my first (and only) breaking-and-entering.

One thing I learned, however, I didn't know what to do with:
Death is into the water, life is the coming out.
I still don't, though nothing else matters but that, it seems,
                            nothing even comes close.

———————

Elm Grove, Pine Valley and Cedar Hill,
                              what detritus one remembers—
The one-armed soldier we spied on making out in the sedge grass
With his red-haired girl friend behind the Elm Grove playground,

For instance, in 1944 . . . I was nine, the fourth grade . . .
I remember telling Brooklyn, my best friend,
                              my dick was stiff all night.
Nine years old! My dick! All night!

We talked about it for days,
                              Oak Ridge abstracted and elsewhere,
—D-Day and Normandy come and gone—
All eyes on the new world's sun king,
                              its rising up and its going down.

———————

It's Wednesday afternoon, and Carter and I are on the road
For the Sullivan County National Bank Loan Department,
1957, Gate City and Southwest Virginia.

We're after deadbeats, delinquent note payers, in Carter's words.
Cemetery plots—ten dollars a month until you die or pay up.
In four months I'll enter the Army, right now I'm Dr. Death,

Riding shotgun for Carter, bringing more misery to the miserable.
Up-hollow and down-creek, shack after unelectrified shack—
The worst job in the world, and we're the two worst people in it.

———————

Overcast afternoon, then weak sun, then overcast again.
A little wind
              whiffles across the back yard like a squall line
In miniature, thumping the clover heads, startling the grass.

11

My parents' 60th wedding anniversary
Were they still alive,

                        5th of June, 1994.
It's hard to imagine, I think, your own children grown older than
    you ever were, I can't.

I sit in one of the knock-off Brown-Jordan deck chairs we
    brought from California,
Next to the bearded grandson my mother never saw.
Some afternoon, or noon, it will all be over. Not this one.

III

June is a migraine above the eyes,
Strict auras and yellow blots,
                    green screen and tunnel vision,
Slow ripples of otherworldliness,

Humidity's painfall drop by drop.
Next door, high whine of the pest exterminator's blunt machine.
Down the street, tide-slap of hammer-and-nail,
                    hammer-and-nail from a neighbor's roof.

I've had these for forty years,
                    light-prints and shifting screed,
Feckless illuminations.
St. John of the Cross, Julian of Norwich, lead me home.

———————

It's good to know certain things:
What's departed, in order to know what's left to come;
That water's immeasurable and incomprehensible

And blows in the air
Where all that's fallen and silent becomes invisible;
That fire's the light our names are carved in.

That shame is a garment of sorrow;
That time is the Adversary, and stays sleepless and wants for

nothing;
That clouds are unequal and words are.

———————

I sense a certain uncertainty in the pine trees,
Seasonal discontent,
                    quotidian surliness,
Pre-solstice jitters, that threatens to rattle our equilibrium.

My friend has lost his larynx,
My friend who in the old days, with a sentence or two,
Would easily set things right,

His glasses light-blanks as he quoted a stanza from Stevens or
          Yeats
Behind his cigarette smoke.
Life's hard, our mutual third friend says . . . It is. It is.

———————

Sundays define me.
                    Born on a back-lit Sunday, like today,
But later, in August,
And elsewhere, in Tennessee, Sundays dismantle me.

There is a solitude about Sunday afternoons
In small towns, surrounded by all that's familiar
And of necessity dear,

That chills us on hot days, like today, unto the grave,
When the sun is a tongued wafer behind the clouds, out of sight,
And wind chords work through the loose-roofed yard sheds,
                                        a celestial music . . .

———————

There is forgetfulness in me which makes me descend
Into a great ignorance,
And makes me to walk in mud, though what I remember remains.

Some of the things I have forgotten:
Who the Illuminator is, and what he illuminates;
Who will have pity on what needs have pity on it.

What I remember redeems me,
                              strips me and brings me to rest,
An end to what has begun,
A beginning to what is about to be ended.

———————

What are the determining moments of our lives?
                              How do we know them?
Are they ends of things or beginnings?
Are we more or less of ourselves once they've come and gone?

I think this is one of mine tonight,
The Turkish moon and its one star
                              crisp as a new flag
Over my hometown street with its dark trash cans looming along
    the curb.

Surely this must be one. And what of me afterwards
When the moon and her sanguine consort
Have slipped the horizon? What will become of me then?

———————

Some names are everywhere—they are above and they are below,
They are concealed and they are revealed.
We call them wise, for the wisdom of death is called the little
    wisdom.

And my name? And your name?
                    Where will we find them, in what pocket?
Wherever it is, better to keep them there not known—
Words speak for themselves, anonymity speaks for itself.

The Unknown Master of the Pure Poem walks nightly among his
        roses,
The very garden his son laid out.
Every so often he sits down. Every so often he stands back up . . .

————————

Heavy, heavy, heavy hangs over our heads. June heat.
How many lives does it take to fabricate this one?
Aluminum pie pan bird frightener
                        dazzles and feints in a desultory breeze

Across the road, vegetable garden mojo, evil eye.
That's one life I know for sure.
Others, like insects in amber,
                    lie golden and lurking and hidden from us.

Ninety-four in the shade, humidity huge and inseparable,
Noon sun like a laser disk.
The grackle waddles forth in his suit of lights,
                            the crucifixion on his back.

————————

Affection's the absolute
                    everything rises to,
Devotion's detail, the sum of all our scatterings,
Bright imprint our lives unshadow on.

Easy enough to say that now, the hush of late spring
Hung like an after-echo

Over the neighborhood,
                            devolving and disappearing.

Easy enough, perhaps, but still true,
Honeysuckle and poison ivy jumbling out of the hedge,
Magnolia beak and white tongue, landscape's off-load, love's lisp.

ENVOI

What we once liked, we no longer like.
What we used to delight in settles like fine ash on our tongues.
What we once embraced embraces us.

Things have destinies, of course,
On-lines and downloads mysterious as the language of clouds.
My life has become like that,

Half uninterpretable, half new geography,
Landscapes stilled and adumbrated, memory unratcheting,
Its voice-over not my own.

Meanwhile, the mole goes on with its subterranean daydreams,
The dogs lie around like rugs,
Birds nitpick their pinfeathers, insects slick down their shells.

No horizon-honing here, no angst in the anthill.
What happens is what happens,
And what happened to happen never existed to start with.

Still, who wants a life like that,
No next and no before, no yesterday, no today,
Tomorrow a moment no one will ever live in?

As for me, I'll take whatever wanes,
The loosening traffic on the straightaway, the dark and such,

The wandering stars, wherever they come from now, wherever
    they go.

I'll take whatever breaks down beneath its own sad weight—
The paintings of Albert Pinkham Ryder, for instance,
Language, the weather, the word of God.

I'll take as icon and testament
The daytime metaphysics of the natural world,
Sun on tie post, rock on rock.

2

POEM HALF IN THE MANNER OF LI HO

All things aspire to weightlessness,
            some place beyond the lip of language,
Some silence, some zone of grace,

Sky white as raw silk,
                    opening mirror cold-sprung in the west,
Sunset like dead grass.

If God hurt the way we hurt,
                    he, too, would be heart-sore,
Disconsolate, unappeasable.

Li Ho, the story goes, would leave home
Each day at dawn, riding a colt, a servant boy
                            walking behind him,
An antique tapestry bag
Strapped to his back.
                    When inspiration struck, Ho would write
The lines down and drop them in the bag.
At night he'd go home and work the lines up into a poem,
No matter how disconnected and loose-leafed they were.
His mother once said,
"He won't stop until he has vomited out his heart."

And so he did.
            Like John Keats,
He died believing his name would never be written among the
    Characters.

Without hope, he thought himself—that worst curse—unlucky.
At twenty-seven, at death's line, he saw a man come
In purple, driving a red dragon,
A tablet in one hand, who said,
                              "I'm here to summon Li Ho."
Ho got from his bed and wept.
Far from the sick room's dragon-dark, snow stormed the passes,
Monkeys surfed the bo trees
                              and foolish men ate white jade.

How mournful the southern hills are,
                              how white their despair
Under December's T'ang blue blank page.

What's the use of words—there are no words
For December's chill redaction,
                              for the way it makes us feel.

We hang like clouds between heaven and earth,
                              between something and nothing,
Sometimes with shadows, sometimes without.

MEDITATION ON FORM AND MEASURE

A palm print confirms the stars, but what confirms the hand?
Out of any two thoughts I have, one is devoted to death.
Our days an uncertainty, a chaos and shapeless,
All that our lives are
                        blurs down, like a landscape reflected in water.
All stars are lights, all lights are not stars.

13 July, buck robin dry-preens on lodge pole branch,
North sky racked-over to stone-washed blue,
Star-wheels in whiteout,
One cloud over Caribou as though spray-painted there,
Doe bird tail-up under stained glass Venetian footbridge.

_____

Spruce-cloister abbeyesque, trees monk-like and shadow-frocked,
Grouse in the dark folds,
Sunlight pale cross through the thick branches,
Male grouse twice-graced in a sacrificial strut,
                        fantailed, away
From something hidden and too young, lord down the dead log.

The moon, like some albino black hole, draws the light in,
The crescent moon, falling and golden,
And darkens the sky around it erupting in stars,
Word stars, warrior stars, word warriors
                        assembling
Accents and destinies, moon drawing the light inside.

_____

Time and light are the same thing somewhere behind our backs.
And form is measure.
                    Without measure there is no form:
Form and measure become one.
Time and light become one somewhere beyond our future.
Father darkness, mother night,
                    one and one become one again.

Now, in their separateness, however, they sizzle and hum,
Sweet, self-destructive music
That cradles our bodies and turns them
Back to an attitude, a near-truth
Where measure is verbal architecture
                    and form is splendor.

                    ———————

Immodestly, we pattern ourselves against the dead,
Echoes and mirrors, distant thunder,
Those fabulous constellations
                    we gaze at but can't explain.
Our lives reflections of shadows, cries
Echoes of echoes, we live among ghosts, sighting and sizing,

Hawk like a circling scrap of ash on the thermal's flame,
Gray jay non grata at feeder trough,
Barn swallows veering like fighter planes
                    out of the overcast,
La Traviata incongruous
Inside from the boom box tape, bird snarl and aria.

                    ———————

Memory is a cemetery
I've visited once or twice, white
                    ubiquitous and the set-aside

Everywhere under foot,
Jack robin back on his bowed branch, missus tucked butt-up
Over the eggs,
             clouds slow and deep as liners over the earth.

My life, like others' lives, has been circumscribed by stars.
O *vaghe stelle dell'orso,*
             beautiful stars of the Bear,
I took, one time, from a book.
Tonight, I take it again, that I, like Leopardi, might
One day immerse myself in its cold, Lethean shine.

POEM ALMOST WHOLLY IN MY

OWN MANNER

Where the Southern cross the Yellow Dog
In Moorhead, Mississippi,
                    my mother sheltered her life out

In Leland, a few miles down US 82,
                         unfretted and unaware,
Layered between history and a three-line lament

About to be brought forth
                    on the wrong side of the tracks
All over the state and the Deep South.

We all know what happened next,
                    blues and jazz and rhythm-and-blues,
Then rock-and-roll, then sex-and-drugs-and-rock-and-roll, lick by
        lick

Blowing the lanterns out—and everything else—along the levees:
Cotton went west, the music went north
                    and everywhere in between,

Time, like a burning wheel, scorching along by the highway
        side,
Reorganizing, relayering,
                    turning the tenants out.

———

9 p.m. August sky eleemosynary, such sweet grief,
Music the distant thunder chord
                          that shudders our lives.

Black notes. The black notes
That follow our footsteps like blood from a cut finger.
                                              Like that.

Fireflies, slow angel eyes,
                    nod and weave,
Tracking our chary attitudes, our malevolent mercies.

Charity, sometimes, we have,
                      appearing and disappearing
Like stars when nightwash rises through us.

(Hope and faith we lip-sync,
                      a dark dharma, a goat grace,
A grace like rain, that goes where rain goes.)

Discreetly the evening enters us,
                          overwhelms us,
As out here whatever lifts, whatever lowers, intersects.

Interstices. We live in the cracks.
Under Ezekiel and his prophesies,
                        under the wheel.

Poetry's what's left between the lines—
                      a strange speech and a hard language,
It's all in the unwritten, it's all in the unsaid . . .

And that's a comfort, I think,

                            for our lack and inarticulation.

For our scalded flesh and our singed hair.

But what would Robert Johnson say,

                            hell-hounded and brimstone-tongued?

What would W. C. Handy say,

Those whom the wheel has overturned,

                            those whom the fire has,

And the wind has, unstuck and unstrung?

They'd say what my mother said—

                            a comfort, perhaps, but too cold

Where the Southern cross the Yellow Dog.

MEDITATION ON SUMMER AND

SHAPELESSNESS

We have a bat, one bat, that bug-surfs
                          our late-summer back yard
Just as the fireflies begin
To rise, new souls, toward the August moon.
Flap-limbed, ungathered,
He stumbles unerringly through them,
Exempt as they feint and ascend to their remission—
Light, Catharist light;
Brightness to brightness where I sit
                          on the back brink of my sixth decade,
Virginia moon in the cloud-ragged, cloud-scutted sky,
Bat bug-drawn and swallow-crossed, God's wash.

One comes to understand
                          Candide and Tiberius,
Sour saints, aspiring aphasiacs,
Recluses and anchorites,
Those whom the moon's pull and the moon's
                          hydrointerpretation
Crumble twice under,
Those hard few for whom the Eagle has never landed.
Out here, all's mythic, medieval, or early A.D.
One half expects
                          Raymond of Toulouse or Hadrian to step forth,
Resplendent and otherwise, out of the hedge row or arborvitae.
One half hopes, moon's gun with a dead bead.

———————

I never quite got it, what they meant,
                              but now I do,
Waking each morning at dawn,
Or before, some shapeless, unfingerprintable dread
On me like cold-crossed humidity,
Extinction shouldering, like a season, in from my dreamscape.
Without my glasses, the light around the window shade
Throbs like an aura, so faint
At first, then luminous with its broken promises—
Feckless icon, dark reliquary.
Mortality hunches, like fine furniture, crowding the room.

Rising, feeding the dogs, bringing the newspaper in,
Somehow should loosen things up.
It doesn't, of course.
                    There's still the pill to be taken,
And then another, eye drops,
Toothbrush and toothpaste,
                    reflection of someone older and strange
Constantly in the mirror,
Breakfast and then the day's doom, long-leafed
And everywhere,
Shadowing what I look at, shadowing what I see.
The News, then supper, then back to the black beginning.

————————

Après-dog days, dead end of August,
Summer a holding pattern,
                    heat, haze, humidity
The mantra we still chant, the bell-tick our tongues all toll.
Whatever rises becomes a light—
Firefly and new moon,
Star and star and star chart
                    unscrolled across the heavens

Like radioactive dump sites bulb-lit on a map.
Whatever holds back goes dark—
The landscape and all its accoutrements, my instinct, my hands,
My late, untouchable hands.

Summer's crepuscular, rot and wrack,
Rain-ravaged, root-ruined.
Each August the nightscape inserts itself
                                          another inch in my heart,
Piece and a piece, piecemeal, time's piecework.
August unedges and polishes me, water's way.
Such subtle lapidary.
Last lights go out in the next door house,
                              dogs disappear,
Privet and white pine go under, bird-squelch and frog-shrill.
To be separate, to be apart, is to be whole again.
Full night now and dust sheet—
                         the happy life is the darkened life.

Sunday, September Sunday . . . Outdoors,
Like an early page from The Appalachian Book of the Dead,
Sunlight lavishes brilliance on every surface,
Doves settle, surreptitious angels, on tree limb and box branch,
A crow calls, deep in its own darkness,
Something like water ticks on
Just there, beyond the horizon, just there, steady clock . . .

Go in fear of abstractions . . .
                              Well, possibly. Meanwhile,
They *are* the strata our bodies rise through, the sere veins
Our skins rub off on.
For instance, whatever enlightenment there might be
Housels compassion and affection, those two tributaries
That river above our lives,
Whose waters we sense the sense of
                              late at night, and later still.

Uneasy, suburbanized,
I drift from the lawn chair to the back porch to the dwarf orchard
Testing the grass and border garden.
A stillness, as in the passageways of Paradise,
Bell jars the afternoon.
                    Leaves, like *ex votos*, hang hard and shine
Under the endlessness of heaven.
Such skeletal altars, such vacant sanctuary.

It always amazes me
How landscape recalibrates the stations of the dead,

How what we see jacks up
                         the odd quotient of what we don't see,
How God's breath reconstitutes our walking up and walking down.
First glimpse of autumn, stretched tight and snicked, a bad face
    lift,
Flicks in and flicks out,
                         a virtual reality.
Time to begin the long division.

3

UMBRIAN DREAMS

Nothing is flat-lit and tabula rasaed in Charlottesville,
Umbrian sackcloth,
                    stigmata and *Stabat mater*,
A sleep and a death away,
Night, and a sleep and a death away—
Light's frost-fired and Byzantine here,
                              aureate, beehived,
Falling in Heraclitean streams
Through my neighbor's maple trees.
There's nothing medieval and two-dimensional in our town,
October in full drag, Mycenaean masked and golden lobed.

Like Yeats, however, I dream of a mythic body,
Feathered and white, a landscape
                    horizoned and honed as an anchorite.
(Iacopo, hear me out, St. Francis, have you a word for me?)
Umbrian lightfall, lambent and ichorous, mists through my days,
As though a wound, somewhere and luminous,
                              flickered and went out,
Flickered and went back out—
So weightless the light, so stretched and pained,
It seems to ooze, and then not ooze, down from that one hurt.
You doubt it? Look. Put your finger there. No, there. You see?

OCTOBER II

October in mission creep,
                       autumnal reprise and stand down.
The more reality takes shape, the more it loses intensity—
Synaptic uncertainty,
Electrical surge and quick lick of the minus sign,
Tightening of the force field
Wherein our forms are shaped and shapes formed,
                   wherein we pare ourselves to our attitudes . . .

Do not despair—one of the thieves was saved; do not presume—
     one of the thieves was damned,
Wrote Beckett, quoting St. Augustine.
It was the shape of the sentence he liked, the double iambic
     pentameter:
It is the shape that matters, he said.
Indeed, shape precludes shapelessness, as God precludes
     Godlessness.
Form is the absence of all things. Like sin. Yes, like sin.

It's the shape beneath the shape that summons us, the juice
That spreads the rose, the multifoliate spark
                   that drops the leaf
And darkens our entranceways,
The rush that transfigures the maple tree,
             the rush that transubstantiates our lives.
October, the season's signature and garnishee,
October, the exponential negative, the plus.

LIVES OF THE SAINTS

1

A loose knot in a short rope,
My life keeps sliding out from under me, intact but
Diminishing,
           its pattern becoming patternless,
The blue abyss of everyday air
Breathing it in and breathing it out,
                                      in little clouds like smoke,
In little wind strings and threads.

Everything that the pencil says is erasable,
Unlike our voices, whose words are black and permanent,
Smudging our lives like coal dust,
                                   unlike our memories,
Etched like a skyline against the mind,
Unlike our irretrievable deeds . . .
The pencil spills everything, and then takes everything back.

For instance, here I am at Hollywood Boulevard and Vine,
Almost 60, Christmas Eve, the flesh-flashers and pimps
And inexhaustible Walk of Famers
                                 snubbing their joints out,
Hoping for something not-too-horrible to happen across the
     street.
The rain squall has sucked up and bumped off,
The palm fronds dangle lubriciously.
                              Life, as they say, is beautiful.

41

2

One week into 1995, and all I've thought about
Is endings, retreads,
                        the love of loss
Light as a locket around my neck, idea of absence
Hard and bright as a dime inside my trouser pocket.
Where is the new and negotiable,
The undiscovered snapshot,
                        the phoneme's refusal, word's rest?

Remember, face the facts, Miss Stein said.
                                            And so I've tried,
Pretending there's nothing there but description, hoping emotion
      shows;
That that's why description's there:
The subject was never smoke,
                        there's always been a fire.
The winter dark shatters around us like broken glass.
The morning sky opens its pink robe.

All explorers must die of heartbreak.
                                    Middle-aged poets, too,
Wind from the northwest, small wind,
Two crows in the ash tree, one on an oak limb across the street.
Endless effortless nothingness, January blue:
Noteless measureless music;
                        imageless iconography.
I'll be the lookout and listener, you do the talking . . .

3

Chinook, the January thaw;
                            warm wind from the Gulf
Spinning the turn-around and dead leaves
Northeast and southeast—
I like it under the trees in winter,
                            everything over me dead,
Or half-dead, sky hard,
Wind moving the leaves around clockwise, then counterclockwise
    too.

We live in a place that is not our own . . .
                            I'll say . . . Roses rot
In the side garden's meltdown, shrubs bud,
The sounds of syllables altogether elsewhere rise
Like white paint through the sun—
                            familiar only with God,
We yearn to be pierced by that
Occasional void through which the supernatural flows.

The plain geometry of the dead does not equate,
Infinite numbers, untidy sums:
We believe in belief but don't believe,
                            for which we shall be judged.
In winter, under the winter trees—
A murder of crows glides over, some thirty or more,
To its appointment,
                    sine and cosine, angle and arc.

4

The winter wind re-nails me,
                              respirations of the divine
In and out, a cold fusion.
Such dire lungs.
The sun goes up and the sun goes down,
                              small yelps from the short weeds.
Listen up, Lord, listen up.
The night birds sleep with their wings ajar.
                              Black branches, black branches.

Al poco giorno ed al gran cerchio d'ombra—
A little light and a great darkness,
Darkness wherein our friends are hid,
                              and our love's gone wrong.
If death is abstract (force through pure, illusory space),
May I be put, when the time comes, in the dwelling of St. John
As I wrest myself from joy
                    into the meta-optics of desire.

Posteriori Dei . . .
God's back, love's loss, light's blank the eye can accommodate
And the heart shelve,
                    world's ever-more-disappearing vacancy
Under the slow-drag clouds of heaven
The landscape absorbs and then repents of,
                              clouds ponderous as a negative
Nothing can keep from moving.

5

The afternoon is urban, and somewhat imaginary,
Behind the snowfall, winter's printout
And self-defense, its matrix and self-design.

                                   All afternoon
The afternoon was ordinary
And self-perpetuating behind its Chinese screen.
But it was urban, and actual, in the long run.

In dread we stay and in dread depart . . .

                                   Not much wrench room.
The 13th century knew this, a movable floor—
Here's bad and There's worse.
Outside the door, demons writhed just under the earth's crust,
Outside the door,
                  and licensed to govern in God's name.
On the street, the ride-bys and executions lip-chant and sing.

Contemplative, cloistered, tongue-tied,
                              Zen says, watch your front.
Zen says, wherever you are is a monastery.
The afternoon says, life's a loose knot in a short rope.
The afternoon says,
                  show me your hands, show me your feet.
The lives of the saints become our lives.
God says, watch your back.

So autumn comes to an end with these few wet sad stains
Stuck to the landscape,
                                    December dark
Running its hands through the lank hair of late afternoon,
Little tongues of the rain holding forth
                                    under the eaves,
Such wash, such watery words . . .

So autumn comes to this end,
And winter's vocabulary, downsized and distanced,
Drop by drop
Captures the conversation with its monosyllabic gutturals
And tin music,
                        gravelly consonants, scratched vowels.

Soon the camel drivers will light their fires, soon the stars
Will start on their brief dip down from the back of heaven,
Down to the desert's dispensation
And night reaches, the gall and first birth,
The second only one word from now,
                                    one word and its death from right now.

Meanwhile, in Charlottesville, the half-moon
Hums like a Hottentot
                        high over Monticello,
Clouds dishevel and rag out,
The alphabet of our discontent
Keeps on with its lettering,
                        gold on the black walls of our hearts . . .

NEGATIVES II

One erases only in order to write again . . .

You don't know what you don't know,
We used to say in the CIC in Verona—
Negative space, negative operability
To counterposition the white drift of the unknown.
You can't see what you can't see.

It's still the best advice, but easy to overlook
As winter grinds out its cigarette
Across the landscape.
                    February.
Who could have known, in 1959, the balloon would not go up?
Who could have seen, back then, the new world's new disorder?

John Ruskin says all clouds are masses of light, even the darkest ones.
Hard to remember that these overcast afternoons,
Midweek, ash-black and ash-white,
                                    negative shapes sketched in
And luminous here and there in loose interstices
Elbowed and stacked between earth and sky.

Hard to remember that as the slipstream of memory shifts
And shutters, massing what wasn't there as though it were.
Where are the secret codes these days for nuking the Brenner Pass?
And the Run, and the Trieste Station?
Like sculptured mist, sharp-edged and cut into form, they slide on by.

One only writes in order to erase again . . .

LIVES OF THE ARTISTS

1

Learn how to model before you learn to finish things,
Michelangelo hisses . . .
                              Before you bear witness,
Be sure you have something that calls for a witnessing,
I might add—
Don't gloss what isn't assignable or brought to bear,
Don't shine what's expendable.

March in the northern south. Hard ides-heat
Bangs through the branches of winter trees,
                                    thumps the gauges
Needling green and immodestly
Out of the dead leaves, out of their opium half-dreams.
Willows, medusa-hooded and bone-browed, begin to swim up
Through their brown depths, wasps revive
                              and plants practice their scales.

In Poussin's apocalypse,
                    we're all merely emanations sent forth
From landscape's hell-hung heart-screen—
Some flee through the dust, some find them a bed in the wind's
    scorched mouth,
Some disappear in flame . . .
                    As I do this afternoon
Under the little fires in the plum tree, white-into-white-into-
    white,
Unidentified bird on a limb, lung-light not of this world.

2

When you have died there will be nothing—
No memory of you will remain,

                              not even a trace as you walk
Aimlessly, unseen, in the fitful halls of the dead,
Sappho warns us. She also writes:
The moon has set, and the Pleiades—

                              in the deep middle of the night
The time is passing . . .

How is it that no one remembers this?

                              Time's ashes, *I lie alone.*
So simple, so simple, so unlike the plastic ticking Christ
Who preyed on us we prayed to—
Such eucharistic side-bars, such saint-shortened anomalies
Under the dull stained glass,

                              down the two-lane and four-lane highways.
Pain enters me drop by drop.

The two plum trees, like tired angels, have *dropped their wings at*
     their sides.
I walk quietly among the autumn offerings
Dark hands from the underworld
Push up around me,

                    gold-amber cups
and bittersweet, nightshade, indulgences from the dead.
I walk quietly and carefully on their altar,

                              among their prayers.

3

We all rise, if we rise at all, to what we're drawn by,
Big Smoke, simplicity's signature,
Last untranslatable text—
The faithful do not speak many words . . .
                                                    What's there to say,
Little smoke, cloud-smoke, in the plum trees,
Something's name indecipherable
                                    rechalked in the scrawled branches.

Everything God possesses, it's been said, *the wise man already
        has.*
Some slack, then, some hope.
Don't give the word to everyone,
The gift is tiny, the world made up
Of deceivers and those who are deceived—
                                                    the true word
Is the word about the word.

Celestial gossip, celestial similes
(Like, like, like, like, like)
Powder the plum blossoms nervously, invisibly,
                                                    the word
In hiding, unstirred. The facts,
The bits of narrative,
                        glow, intermittent and flaked.
The sins of the uninformed are the first shame of their teachers.

4

Jaundicing down from their purity, the plum blossoms
Snowfall out of the two trees
And spread like a sheet of mayflies
                              soundlessly, thick underfoot—
I am the silence that is incomprehensible,
First snow stars drifting down from the sky,
                              late fall in the other world;
I am the utterance of my name.

Belief in transcendence,
                    belief in something beyond belief,
Is what the blossoms solidify
In their fall through the two worlds—
The imaging of the invisible, the slow dream of metaphor,
Sanction our going up and our going down, our days
And the lives we infold inside them,
                              our *yes* and *yes.*

Good to get that said, tongue of cold air
Licking the landscape,
                    snuffing the flame in the green fuse.
I am the speech that cannot be grasped.
I am the substance and the thing that has no substance,
Cast forth upon the face of the earth,
Whose margins we write in,
                    whose one story we tell, and keep on telling.

5

There's nothing out there but light,

the would-be artist said,

As usual just half right:
There's also a touch of darkness, everyone knows, on both sides
    of both horizons,
Prescribed and unpaintable,
Touching our fingertips whichever way we decide to jump.
His small palette, however, won't hold that color,

though some have, and some still do.

The two plum trees know nothing of that,
Having come to their green grief,

their terrestrial touch-and-go,

Out of grace and radiance,
Their altered bodies alteration transmogrified.
Mine is a brief voice, a still, brief voice
Unsubject to change or the will to change—

might it be restrung and rearranged.

But that is another story.

Vasari tells us

An earlier tale than Greek of the invention of painting,
How Gyges of Lydia
Once saw his own shadow cast

by the light of a fire

And instantly drew his own outline on the wall with charcoal . . .
Learn to model before you learn how to finish things.

DEEP MEASURE

Shank of the afternoon, wan weight-light,
Undercard of a short month,
                              February Sunday . . .
Wordlessness of the wrong world.
In the day's dark niche, the patron saint of What-Goes-Down
Shuffles her golden deck and deals,
                              one for you and one for me . . .

And that's it, a single number—we play what we get.
My hand says measure,
                              doves on the wire and first bulb blades
Edging up through the mulch mat,
Inside-out of the winter gum trees,
A cold harbor, cold stop and two-step, and here it comes,

Deep measure,
                    deep measure that runnels beneath the bone,
That sways our attitude and sets our lives to music;
Deep measure, down under and death-drawn:
Pilgrim, homeboy of false time,
Listen and set your foot down,
                              listen and step lightly.

THINKING OF WINTER

AT THE BEGINNING OF SUMMER

Milton paints purple trees. Avery.
                              And Wolf Kahn too.
I've liked their landscapes,
Nightdreams and daymares,
                              pastures and woods that burn our eyes.
Otherwise, why would we look?
Otherwise, why would we stretch our hands out and gather them
     in?

My brother slides through the blue zones in enormous planes.
My sister's cartilage, ash and bone.
My parents rock in their blackened boats
                              back and forth, back and forth.
Above the ornamental cherries, the sky is a box and a glaze.
Well, yes, a box and a glaze.

Pulled from despair like a bad tooth,
I see my roots, tiny roots,
                              glisten like good luck in the sun.
What we refuse defines us,
                              a little of this, a little of that.
The light stays fool's gold for a long time.
The light stays fool's gold for a long time.

                                        —For Winter Wright

4

JESUIT GRAVES

Midsummer. Irish overcast. Oatmeal-colored sky.
The Jesuit pit. Last mass
For hundreds whose names are incised on the marble wall
Above the gravel and grassless dirt.
Just dirt and the small stones—
                                how strict, how self-effacing.

Not suited for you, however, Father Bird-of-Paradise,
Whose *plumage of far wonder* is not formless and not faceless,
Whatever you might have hoped for once.
Glasnevin Cemetery, Dublin, 3 July 1995.
For those who would rise to meet their work,
                                that work is scaffolding.

Sacrifice is the cause of ruin.
The absence of sacrifice is the cause of ruin.
Thus the legends instruct us,
North wind through the flat-leaved limbs of the sheltering trees,
Three desperate mounds in the small, square enclosure,
                                souls God-gulped and heaven-hidden.

P. Gerardus Hopkins, 28 July 1844–8 June 1889, Age 44.
And then the next name. And then the next,
Soldiers of misfortune, lock-step into a star-colored tight dissolve,
History's hand-me-ons. But you, Father Candescence,
You, Father Fire?
                    Whatever rises comes together, they say. They say.

57

I love to wake to the *coo coo* of the mourning dove
At dawn—
        like one drug masking another's ill effects,
It tells me that everything's all right when I know that
    everything's wrong.
It lays out the landscape's hash marks,
                    the structures of everyday.
It makes what's darkened unworkable
For that moment, and that, as someone once said, is grace.
But this bird's a different story.

Dawn in the Umbrian hills.
In the cracks of the persian blinds, slim ingots of daylight stack
    and drip.
This bird has something to say—
                 a watery kind of music,
Extended improvisations, liquid riffs and breaks—
But not to me, pulled like a dead weight
From the riptide of sleep, not to me,
Depression's darling, history's hand job, not to me . . .

———

Twice, now, I've heard the nightingale.
                First in the first light
Of a dust-grey dawn,
And then at midnight, a week later,
Walking my friend to the parking lot
In Todi, moon vamping behind the silted cloud mounds,
A pentimento of sudden illumination,

58

Like bird work or spider work.

                    Senti, my friend said, *Shhh,*

È *l'usignolo,* the nightingale,
As bird and bird song drifted downhill,

                       easy as watershine,
Ripply and rock-run.
Silence. No moon, no motorbike, no bird.
The silence of something come and something gone away.
Nightingale, ghost bird, ghost song,
Hand that needles and threads the night together,

                        light a candle for me.

———————

Swallows over the battlements

                 and thigh-moulded red tile roofs,
Square crenelations, Guelph town.
Swallows against the enfrescoed backdrop of tilled hills
Like tiny sharks in the tinted air
That buoys them like a tide,

                 arrested, water-colored surge.
Swallows darting like fish through the alabaster air,
Cleansing the cleanliness, feeding on seen and the unseen.

To come back as one of them!
Loose in the light and landscape-shine,

                 language without words,
Ineffable part of the painting and ignorant of it,
Pulled by the lunar landswell,
Demi-denizen of the godhead
Spread like a golden tablecloth wherever you turn—
Such judgment, such sweet witch-work.

———————

This mockingbird's got his chops.
Bird song over black water—
Am I south or north of my own death,

                          west or east of my final hurt?
In North Carolina, half a century ago,
Bird song over black water,
Lake Llewellyn Bibled and night-colored,

                         mockingbird
Soul-throated, like light, a little light in great darkness.

Zodiac damped, then clicked off,

                    cloud-covering-heaven.
Bird song over black water.
I remember the way the song contained many songs,
As it does now, the same song
Over the tide pool of my neighbor's yard, and mine's slack
    turning,
Many songs, a season's worth,
Many voices, a light to lead back

                  to silence, sound of the first voice.

———————

Medieval, prelatic, why
Does the male cardinal sing that song, *omit, omit,*
From the eminence of the gum tree?
What is it he knows,

               silence, *omit, omit,* silence,
The afternoon breaking away in little pieces,
Siren's squeal from the bypass,
The void's tattoo, *Nothing Matters,*

             mottoed across our white hearts?

Nature abhors originality, according to Cioran.
Landscape desires it, I say,

The back yard unloading its cargo of solitudes
Into the backwash of last light—
Cardinal, exhale my sins,

                        help me to lie low and leave out,
Remind me that vision is singular, that excess
Is regress, that more than enough is too much, that

                                        compression is all.

SITTING AT DUSK IN THE BACK YARD

AFTER THE MONDRIAN RETROSPECTIVE

Form imposes, structure allows—
                              the slow destruction of form
So as to bring it back resheveled, reorganized,
Is the hard heart of the enterprise.
                              Under its camouflage,
The light, relentless shill and cross-dresser, pools and deals.
Inside its short skin, the darkness burns.

Mondrian thought the destructive element in art
Much too neglected.
                    Landscape, of course, pursues it savagely.
And that's what he meant:
You can't reconstruct without the destruction being built in;
There is no essence unless
                          nothing has been left out.

Destruction takes place so order might exist.
                                        Simple enough.
Destruction takes place at the point of maximum awareness.
Orate sine intermissione, St. Paul instructs.
Pray uninterruptedly.
The gods and their names have disappeared.
                                    Only the clouds remain.

Meanwhile, the swallows wheel, the bat wheels, the grackles
      begin their business.
It's August.
          The countryside
Gathers itself for sacrifice, its slow

                        fadeout along the invisible,
Leaving the land its architecture of withdrawal,
Black lines and white spaces, an emptiness primed with reds and
    blues.

BLACK ZODIAC

Darkened by time, the masters, like our memories, mix
And mismatch,
         and settle about our lawn furniture, like air
Without a meaning, like air in its clear nothingness.
What can we say to either of them?
How can they be so dark and so clear at the same time?
They ruffle our hair,
         they ruffle the leaves of the August trees.
Then stop, abruptly as wind.
The flies come back, and the heat—
         what can we say to them?
Nothing is endless but the sky.
The flies come back, and the afternoon
Teeters a bit on its green edges,
         then settles like dead weight
Next to our memories, and the pale hems of the masters' gowns.

———————

Those who look for the Lord will cry out in praise of him.
Perhaps. And perhaps not—
         dust and ashes though we are,
Some will go wordlessly, some
Will listen their way in with their mouths
Where pain puts them, an inch-and-a-half above the floor.
And some will revile him out of love
         and deep disdain.
The gates of mercy, like an eclipse, darken our undersides.
Rows of gravestones stay our steps,
         August humidity

Bright as auras around our bodies.
And some will utter the words,
                              speaking in fear and tongues,
Hating their garments splotched by the flesh.
These are the lucky ones, the shelved ones, the twice-erased.

———————

Dante and John Chrysostom
Might find this afternoon a sidereal roadmap,
A pilgrim's way . . .
                    You might too
Under the prejaundiced outline of the quarter moon,
Clouds sculling downsky like a narrative for *whatever comes*,
What *hasn't happened to happen yet*
Still lurking behind the stars,
                              31 August 1995 . . .
The afterlife of insects, space graffiti, white holes
In the landscape,
                  such things, such avenues, lead to dust
And handle our hurt with ease.
Sky blue, blue of infinity, blue
                              waters above the earth:
Why do the great stories always exist in the past?

———————

The unexamined life's no different from
                              the examined life—
Unanswerable questions, small talk,
Unprovable theorems, long-abandoned arguments—
You've got to write it all down.
Landscape or waterscape, light-length on evergreen, dark sidebar
Of evening,
            you've got to write it down.
Memory's handkerchief, death's dream and automobile,

God's sleep,
                    you've still got to write it down,
Moon half-empty, moon half-full,
Night starless and egoless, night blood-black and prayer-black,
Spider at work between the hedges,
Last bird call,
                    toad in a damp place, tree frog in a dry . . .

—————

We go to our graves with secondary affections,
Second-hand satisfaction, half-souled,
                                        star charts demagnetized.
We go in our best suits. The birds are flying. Clouds pass.
Sure we're cold and untouchable,
                                        but we harbor no ill will.
No tooth tuned to resentment's fork,
                                        we're out of here, and sweet meat.
Calligraphers of the disembodied, God's word-wards,
What letters will we illuminate?
Above us, the atmosphere,
The nothing that's nowhere, signs on, and waits for our beck and
        call.
Above us, the great constellations sidle and wince,
The letters undarken and come forth,
Your X and my X.
                    The letters undarken and they come forth.

—————

Eluders of memory, nocturnal sleep of the greenhouse,
Spirit of slides and silences,
                    Invisible Hand,
Witness and walk on.
Lords of the discontinuous, lords of the little gestures,
Succor my shift and save me . . .

All afternoon the rain has rained down in the mind,
And in the gardens and dwarf orchard.

                                        All afternoon
The lexicon of late summer has turned its pages
Under the rain,

                abstracting the necessary word.
Autumn's upon us.
The rain fills our narrow beds.
Description's an element, like air or water.

                                        That's the word.

CHINA MAIL

It's deep summer east of the Blue Ridge.
Temperatures over 90 for the twenty-fifth day in a row.
The sound of the asphalt trucks down Locust Avenue
Echoes between the limp trees.
                              Nothing's cool to the touch.

Since you have not come,
The way back will stay unknown to you.
And since you have not come,
                              I find I've become like you,
A cloud whose rain has all fallen, adrift and floating.

Walks in the great void are damp and sad.
Late middle age. With little or no work,
                              we return to formlessness,
The beginning of all things.
Study the absolute, your book says. But not too hard,

I add, just under my breath.
Cicadas ratchet their springs up to a full stop
                              in the green wings of the oaks.
This season is called white hair.
Like murdered moonlight, it keeps coming back from the dead.

Our lives will continue to turn unmet,
                              like Virgo and Scorpio.
Of immortality, there's nothing but old age and its aftermath.
It's better you never come.
How else would we keep in touch, tracing our words upon the air?

5

DISJECTA MEMBRA

1

Back yard, dry flower half-border, unpeopled landscape
Stripped of embellishment and anecdotal concern:
A mirror of personality,
                              unworldly and self-effacing,
The onlooker sees himself in,
                              a monk among the oak trees . . .
How silly, the way we place ourselves—the struck postures,
The soothing words, the sleights-of-hand
                              to hoodwink the Paraclete—
For our regard; how always the objects we draw out
To show ourselves to effect
(The chiaroscuro of character we yearn for)
Find us a shade untrue and a shade untied.
                              Bad looking glass, bad things.

————————

Simplify, Shaker down, the voice drones.
Out of the aether, disembodied and discontent,
No doubt who *that* is . . .
                              Autumn prehensile from day one,
Equinox pushing through like a cold front from the west,
Drizzle and dropped clouds, wired wind.
It's Sunday again, brief devotions.
We look down, dead leaves and dead grass like a starry sky
From inside out.
                              Simplify, open the emptiness, divest—
The trees do, each year milking their veins

Down, letting the darkness drip in,
                              I.V. from the infinite.

———————

Filing my nails in the Buddha yard.
Ten feet behind my back, like slow, unsteady water,
Backwash of traffic spikes and falls off,
Zendo half-hunched through the giant privet,
                              shut sure as a shell.
Last cat's-eyes of dew crystal and gold as morning fills the grass.
Between Buddha-stare and potting shed,
Indian file of ants. Robin's abrupt arrival
And dust-down.
                 Everything's one with everything else now,
Wind leaf-lifter and tuck-in,
Light giving over to shadow and shadow to light.

———————

I hope for a second chance where the white clouds are born,
Where the maple trees turn red,
                              redder by half than where
The flowers turned red in spring.
Acolyte at the altar of wind,
I love the idleness of the pine tree,
                              the bright steps into the sky.
I've always wanted to lie there, as though under earth,
Blood drops like sapphires, the dark stations ahead of me
Like postal stops on a deep journey.
I long for that solitude,
                 that rest,
The bed-down and rearrangement of all the heart's threads.

———————

What nurtures us denatures us and will strip us down.
Zen says, stand by the side of your thoughts
As you might stand by the bank of a wide river.
                                        Dew-burdened,
Spider webs spin like little galaxies in the juniper bush,
Morning sunlight corpus delicti
                        sprawled on the damp pavement.
Denatures us to a nub.
And sends us twisting out of our back yards into history.
As though by a wide river,
                        water hustling our wants away,
And what we're given, and what we hope to be absolved of . . .
How simply it moves, how silently.

———————

Death's still the secret of life,
                        the garden reminds us.
Or vice-versa. It's complicated.
Unlike the weed-surge and blossom-surge of early fall,
Unlike the insect husks in the spider's tracery,
Crickets and rogue crows gearing up for afternoon sing-along.
The cottontail hides
                        out in the open, hunched under the apple tree
Between the guillotine of sunlight and guillotine of shade
Beyond my neighbor's hedge.
                        The blades rise and the blades fall,
But rabbit sits tight. Smart bun.
Sit tight and hold on. Sit tight. Hold on.

———————

Love is more talked about than surrendered to. Lie low,
Meng Chiao advises—
                        beauty too close will ruin your life.

Like the south wind, it's better to roam without design.
A lifetime's a solitary thread, we all learn,

and needs its knot tied.
Under the arborvitae,
The squirrels have buried their winter dreams,

and ghosts gather, close to home.
My shadow sticks to the trees' shadow.
There is no simile for this,

this black into black.
Or if there is, it's my penpoint's drop of ink slurred to a word.
Of both, there soon will be not a trace.

———————

With what words, with what silence—
Silence becoming speechlessness,

words being nothing at all—
Can we address a blade of grass, the immensity of a snowflake?
How is it that we presume so much?

There are times, Lord, there are times . . .
We must bite hard into the 21st century,
We must make it bleed.
October approaches the maple trees with its laying-on of hands,
Red stains in the appled west,

red blush beginning to seep through
Just north of north, arterial headway, cloud on cloud.
Let it come, Lord, let it come.

2

If I could slide into a deep sleep,
I could say—to myself, without speaking—why my words
    embarrass me.

Nothing regenerates us, or shapes us again from the dust.
Nothing whispers our name in the night.
Still must we praise you, nothing,
                            still must we call to you.

Our sin is lack of transparency.

November is dark and doom-dangled,
                            fitful bone light
And suppuration, worn wrack
In the trees, dog rot and dead leaves, watch where you're
    going . . .

Illegibility. Dumb fingers from a far hand.

———————

When death completes the number of the body, its food
Is weeping and much groaning,
                            and stranglers come, who roll
Souls down on the dirt . . .
                    And thus it is written, and thus believed,
Though others have found it otherwise.

The restoration of the nature of the ones who are good
Takes place in a time that never had a beginning.

Well, yes, no doubt about that.
One comes to rest in whatever is at rest, and eats
The food he has hungered for.
The light that shines forth there, on that body, does not sink.

————————

This earth is a handful of sleep, eyes open, eyes shut,
A handful, just that—

There is an end to things, but not here.
It's where our names are, hanging like flesh from the flame trees.

Still, there are no flame points in the sky—

There are no angels, there is no light
At just that point where one said,
                              this is where light begins.

It dies out in me.

The word is inscribed in the heart.
                              It is beyond us,
The heart, that changeling, word within word.

————————

Compulsive cameo, God's blue breath
So light on the skin, so infinite,

Why do I have to carry you, unutterable?
Why do you shine out,
                    lost penny, unspendable thing,

Irreversible, unappeasable, luminous,
Recoursed on the far side of language?

Tomorrow's our only hiding place,
November its last address—
                              such small griefs, such capture.

Insurmountable comforts.
And still I carry you. And still you continue to shine out.

———————

Substance. And absence of all substance.
God's not concerned for anything, and has no desire.

Late at night we feel,
                              insensate, immaculata,
The cold, coercive touch of nothing, whose fingerprints
Adhere like watermarks to the skin—

Late at night, our dark and one refuge.

Life is a sore gain, no word, no world.
Eternity drips away, inch by inch, inside us,
December blitzing our blind side,
                              white-tongued and anxious.

That's it. Something licks us up.

———————

December. Blood rolls back to its wound.
God is a scattered part,
                              syllable after syllable, his name asunder.

No first heaven, no second.

Winter sun is a killer,
                late light bladed horizon-like
Wherever you turn,
              arteried, membraned, such soft skin.

Prayers afflict us, this world and the next:

Grief's an eclipse, it comes and it goes.
Photographs show that stars are born as easily as we are.
Both without mercy.

Each leads us away, leads us away.

––––––––––

Guilt is a form in itself.
              As is the love of sentences
That guilt resides in, then darkens.
                  It is as certain.
It is as unregenerative. It is as worn.

Everything terminal has hooks in eternity.
Marsh grass, for instance. Foxfire.
Root work and come-betweens,
                the Lord's welkin and Lord's will,

As some say in these parts not out loud.

In the bare tines of the lemon tree,
Thorns bristle and nubs nudge,
                limbs in a reverie of lost loads.
This life is our set-aside, our dry spot and shelter.

––––––––––

When slant-light crisps up,
                    and shatters like broken lime glass
Through the maple trees, in December,
Who cares about anything but weights and absolutes?

Write up, it's bad, write down, it's still bad.
Remember, everyone's no one.

The abyss of time is a white glove—
                    take it off, put it on,
Finger by finger it always fits,
Buttons mother-of-pearl, so snug, such soft surroundings.

Lord of the broken oak branch,
                    Lord of the avenues,
Tweak and restartle me, guide my hand.

3

Whatever it was I had to say,
                    I've said two times, and then a third.
An object for light to land on,
                    I'm one-on-one with the visible
And shadowy overhang.
It's Christmas Eve, and the Pleiades
Burn like high altar host flames
                    scrunched in the new moon sky—
Their earthly, votive counterparts flash and burst in the spruce
    trees
And Mrs. Fornier's window.
It's 9:10 and I'm walking the dogs down Locust Avenue.
It's a world we've memorized by heart:
Myopic constellations, dog's bark,
                    bleak supplicants, blood of the lamb . . .

———————

Unfinished, unable, distracted—
How easily we reproach ourselves for our lives lived badly,
How easily us undo.
Despair is our consolation, sweet word,
                    and late middle age
And objectivity dulled and drear.
Splendor of little fragments.
Rilke knew one or two things about shame and unhappiness
And how we waste time and worse.
I think I'm starting to catch on myself.

            I think I'm starting to understand
The difference between the adjective and the noun.

———————

Dead moth, old metaphysician, cross-backed, Christ's arrowhead,
    look,
I'll tell you one thing—
Inch by inch, everyday, our lives become less and less.
Obsessive and skinless, we shrink them down.
And here's another—
                a line of poetry's a line of blood.
A cross on the back is like a short sword in the heart,
December sun in a fadeaway, cloud under cloud
Over the Blue Ridge,
                just there, just west of Bremo Bluff.
Okay, I'll keep my mouth shut and my eyes fast on the bare
    limbs of the fruit trees.
A line in the earth's a life.

———————

O well the snow falls and small birds drop out of the sky,
The back yard's a winding sheet—
                winter in Charlottesville,
Epiphany two days gone,
Nothing at large but Broncos, pickups and 4x4s.
Even the almost full moon
                is under a monochrome counterpane
Of dry grey.
            Eve of St. Agnes and then some, I'd say,
Twenty-three inches and coming down.
The Rev. Doctor Syntax puts finger to forehead on the opposite
    wall,
Mancini and I still blurred beside him, Mykonos, 1961,
The past a snowstorm the present too.

The human position—anxiety's afterlife, still place—
Escapes us.
                    We live in the wind-chill,
The what-if and what-was-not,
The blown and sour dust of just after or just before,
The metaquotidian landscape
                              of soft edge and abyss.
How hard to take the hard day and ease it in our hearts,
Its icicle and snowdrift and
                            its wind that keeps on blowing.
How hard to be as human as snow is, or as true,
So sure of its place and many names.
It holds the white light against its body, it benights our eyes.

The poem uncurls me, corrects me and croons my tune,
Its outfit sharp as the pressed horizon.
                              Excessive and honed,
It grins like a blade,
It hums like a fuse,
                    body of ash, body of fire,
A music my ear would be heir to.
I glimpse it now and then through the black branches of winter
    trees.
I hear its burn in the still places.
Halfway through January, sky pure, sky not so pure,
World still in tucker and bib.
Might I slipstream its fiery ride,
                              might I mind its smoke.

Is *this* the life we long for,

to be at ease in the natural world,

Blue rise of Blue Ridge
Indented and absolute through the January oak limbs,
Turkey buzzard at work on road-kill opossum, up
And flapping each time
A car passes and coming back

huge and unfolded, a black bed sheet,

Crows fierce but out of focus high up in the ash tree,
Afternoon light from stage left
Low and listless, little birds
Darting soundlessly back and forth, hush, hush?

Well, yes, I think so.

—————————

Take a loose rein and a deep seat,

John, my father-in-law, would say

To someone starting out on a long journey, meaning, take it
    easy,
Relax, let what's taking you take you.
I think of landscape incessantly,

mountains and rivers, lost lakes

Where sunsets festoon and override,
The scald of summer wheat fields, light-licked and poppy-
    smeared.
Sunlight surrounds me and winter birds

doodle and peck in the dead grass.

I'm emptied, ready to go. Again
I tell myself what I've told myself for almost thirty years—
Listen to John, do what the clouds do.

NOTES

APOLOGIA PRO VITA SUA

The Nag Hammadi Library, James M. Robinson, general editor (New York: Harper and Row, 1988).

LIVES OF THE SAINTS

Walter Raleigh, Gertrude Stein, Wallace Stevens, Dante Alighieri, Adam Gopnik, Bertran de Born, Donald Justice, Robert Graves, Anonymous (early thirteenth century) . . .

LIVES OF THE ARTISTS

The Poems of Sappho, translated by Suzy Q Groden (New York: Bobbs-Merrill, 1966); *The Nag Hammadi Library; Lives of the Artists,* Giorgio Vasari, translated by George Bull (New York: Penguin Books, 1965).

THINKING OF WINTER

AT THE BEGINNING OF SUMMER

Jacques Prévert, "Picasso's Walk."

BLACK ZODIAC

The Ruin of Kasch, Roberto Calasso, translated by William Weaver and Stephen Sartarelli (Cambridge: The Belknap Press of Harvard University Press, 1994); *The Confessions* of St. Augustine, translated by R. S. Pine-Coffin (New York: Penguin Books, 1961); *Poems of Paul Celan,* translated by Michael Hamburger (New York: Persea Books, 1989); "Adagia," Wallace Stevens, from *Opus Posthumous* (New York: Alfred A. Knopf, 1957).

CHINA MAIL

The poems of Tu Fu, various translators . . .

DISJECTA MEMBRA

("These fragments are the *disjecta membra* of an elusive, coveted, and vaguely scented knowledge." Guido Ceronetti, *The Science of the Body*); *Poems of the Late T'ang,* translated by A. C. Graham (New York: Penguin Books, 1965); Letters of Paul Celan to Nelly Sachs; *The Nag Hammadi Library; Poems of Paul Celan.*